Sir Edward Bulwer Lytton

**The National Songs of Servia**

Sir Edward Bulwer Lytton

**The National Songs of Servia**

ISBN/EAN: 9783337265526

Printed in Europe, USA, Canada, Australia, Japan

Cover: Foto ©Thomas Meinert / pixelio.de

More available books at **www.hansebooks.com**

their contents makes them desirable always and everywhere.  The series includes

# STORIES, ESSAYS, SKETCHES, AND POEMS

### SELECTED FROM THE WRITINGS OF

| | |
|---|---|
| *Emerson,* | *Tennyson,* |
| *Longfellow,* | *Lowell,* |
| *Whittier,* | *Holmes,* |
| *Hawthorne,* | *Browning,* |
| *Carlyle,* | *Macaulay,* |
| *Aldrich,* | *Milton,* |
| *Hood,* | *Campbell,* |
| *Gray,* | *Owen Meredith,* |
| *Aytoun,* | *Pope,* |

*Thomson,*

### AND OTHERS OF EQUAL FAME.

The volumes are beautifully printed, many of them illustrated, and bound in flexible cloth covers, at a uniform price of

### FIFTY CENTS EACH.

## JAMES R. OSGOOD & CO.,
### PUBLISHERS, BOSTON.

THE

# National Songs of Servia.

TRANSLATED BY

## OWEN MEREDITH.

Omne meum : nihil meum.

BOSTON:

JAMES R. OSGOOD AND COMPANY,

*Late Ticknor and Fields, and Fields, Osgood, & Co.*

1877.

# INTRODUCTION.

N the following Poems no attempt has been made at accurate verbal translation from the original language. They cannot, indeed, be called translations in the strict sense of the word. What they are, let the reader decide. What they are meant to be, is nothing more than a rude medium through which to convey to other minds something of the impression made upon my own by the poetry of a people amongst whom literature is yet unborn ; who in the nineteenth century retain, with the traditions, many also of the habits and customs, of a barbarous age ; and whose social life represents the struggle of centuries to maintain, under the code of Mahomet, the creed of Christ. It is indeed this strange intermixture of Mahometan with Christian association which gives to the poetry of the Serbs its most striking characteristic. It is the sword of a Crusader in the scabbard of a Turk. That, however, which mainly distinguishes this from all other contemporary poetry with which I am acquainted, is the evidence borne on the face of it of an origin, not in the heads of a few, but in the hearts of all. This is a poetry of which the People is the Poet. The " People," not as representing, in contradistinction to all other constituent parts of a community, that class which lies broadly at the basis of a civilization culminating through many social ranks and orders in a high degree of refinement, but " the People," as expressive of one great nationality, which, however geographically subdivided, is yet in that rude and elementary social condition which consists but of a single class, and admits but one aspect of life, one mode of thought, one series of sensations, one train of association. And as is the people, so is the poetry. It is inferior to the poetry of the Persians inasmuch as it is less intellectual, has less fancy, less wisdom, less art. It is destitute of whatever indicates individual thought or personal observation of life. It has nothing of the graceful fancy which glitters through the Gulistan, and never rises to such sweet and noble tones as those which render harmonious some portions of the Shah Nameh. Here we shall find no trace of that gracious chivalry which Ferdausi, perhaps, bequeathed to Ariosto, and assuredly none of that shrewd and somewhat sad experience of mankind which followed, among the roses of his immortal Garden, Sadi, " the wanderer of the world." But such merits are perhaps incompatible with the poetry in what, of the Serbs, is most remarkable, — I mean, that spontaneity and unity, that evidence of collective inspiration, which has never survived the childhood of a people. Such flowers as grow here may be merely mountain weeds, but the dew of the morning is on them.

There is a period in the early life of every people, before man has been divided into men, when the many are still the one. Special and particular sources of interest are as yet neither sought nor discovered. Popular sympathy exists only for subjects of general history or universal experience; and in regard to these all men feel the same feeling and think the same thought. The individual mind lies yet unformed in the matrix of the general life, and the only individual is the Race. Even the gods belong to it. Whoever, then, is the first to speak aloud has the advantage of speaking for all. He expresses not only his own, but every man's sensations and experience. It follows that there is between the fact and the word a directness, closeness, and simplicity of connection which cannot afterwards be realized. For, of all things in nature, the first description is likely to be the best, because it is the most obvious, and therefore the most generally true. The earth is black, the grass is green, the heaven is high, the sea is deep. To say more about them is, in reality, to say less of them. For, as we cannot extend or vary the Universal, every

word added to that which expresses the permanent
and general quality of a thing can only relate to
what is partial and particular, and, therefore, less
valuable. But so inherent to the thing spoken of
is the attribute first selected to qualify it, that by
the process of universal usage the epithet is soon
absorbed back into the noun. The words "deep
sea" and "black earth" imperceptibly cease to express anything more than "the sea" and "the
earth"; and the modern poet, in order to refresh
the sense of perception, is constrained to designate
these things anew by some epithet which, in pro-
portion as it is original, expresses only a limited
and special experience. It is this primitive *univer-
sality* which gives to the poetry of the Serbs its
freshness and its force. Adopting a word now generally admitted into our vocabulary from the German, I would describe it as especially "objective."
The smallest Servian song is therefore rather dramatic than lyrical. For the lyrical poet necessarily
expresses a subjective state of mind, and the shallow
critic who accuses him of egotism is simply accusing
him of being a lyric poet.

It is so impossible to separate the Servian poetry
from the Servian people, and so difficult to form
any judgment of the former without reference to the
latter, that I entreat the reader's sufferance to say
a few words about the Serbs, preliminary to his
perusal of this attempted reproduction of some of

their songs. Those who edit other men's poems are wont to affix to the poetry an introductory notice of the author. I claim a very brief use of this privilege ; for the Servian people is the author of the Servian poetry.

This people, a branch of the old Slavonic family, descended in the seventh century from the Krapak mountains, and established themselves, under permission of the Emperor Heracleus, in Mesia Superiora. Until 923, Servia formed a small state, with its kings and history but little known. At that epoch it was conquered by the Bulgarians, and soon passed, with them, under the dominion of the Greek emperors. In the twelfth century the Serbs, taking advantage of the weakness of the Lower Empire, rendered themselves independent under Tchoudomil, and founded an empire which, in the fourteenth century, became very powerful under Douchan the Magnanimous, who assumed the title of tzar or emperor.

This empire included a portion of Thrace and Macedonia, and many towns in Thessaly and Albania. Under the reign of Ouroch the First the power of it declined ; and at the battle of Kossovo (15th June, 1389), Lazarus, the last Servian Knès, was destroyed, with his army, by the Sultan Amurath the First. After this fatal day Servia ceased to be a nation. The name of it was effaced from the map of Europe, and the country portioned out into various pachaliks, of which the principal was that of Belgrade, then called the Sandgaciat of Semendria. From this epoch the Serbs remained for four hundred years victims of an oppression so unspeakably bitter that it would be difficult to convey to the mind of a modern European any idea of the intolerable nature of it. Thus subjected to a domination brutal and sanguinary in the extreme, at a period when, throughout Europe, arts, letters, and commerce were on the decline, the people soon lost every vestige of an imperfect civilization. From discouragement they sunk into degradation, — the degradation of a people which has ceased to hope. To escape as much as might be from the sight of their oppressors, they abandoned their towns, and dwelt concealed among the woods and mountains, where they bred and tended swine.

At this day the results of prolonged oppression are unhappily to be traced throughout Servia in all that debases the character and contracts the self-development of a people. That universal worship of the lie which is the creed of the slave, that predisposition to frantic ferocity which is the reaction from suppressed and impotent hatred — insincerity and servility, cunning and cruelty — these are at once the defects of the Servian character and the results of the Turkish rule. The demoralization of the people is sadly to be seen in their poetry. It extols, as a public virtue, treachery to the public foe, mistakes trickery for strategy, falsehood for finesse, cruelty for valor, and admits into the character of a hero every vice save' that of physical cowardice.

In the war declared by Josef II. against the Porte, the Serbs took arms with the Austrians. Accustomed, during that brief period, to the enjoyment of comparative independence, they resolved, after the peace of Sistov, not lightly to part with the blessing of it. About a tenth part of the population withdrew armed, in little bands, into their forests and mountains. These little armed companies, leading amongst their natural mountain fastnesses a marauding migratory life, partly of a predatory, partly of a political character, called themselves Haidouks, or Bandits, and form a social phenomenon not very dissimilar to that represented by the banditti of Marco Sciarra in the forests around mediæval Rome. It is but a very few years since the Haidouk has ceased to be a prominent social feature in Servia. He is a principal personage in the poetry of the people, and Monsieur Dozon, to whose able and interesting little work upon the poetry of the Serbs I am largely indebted,* relates that he

---

* Those who may feel interested to know more of the heroic *pesmas*, will find in this work a faithful though slightly abbreviated prose translation of them, together with an excellent criticism on the poetry of the Serbs, from which I have herein adopted many statements entirely confirmed by my own experience in the country.

was informed by a late Minister of the Interior in Servia, that in certain portions of the principality it had been found necessary to prohibit the recitation of the popular songs about the Haidouks, as numbers of those who listened to them had been incited to adopt the lawless life therein described.

The revolt of the Serbs under Kara-George (or Black George), and the disastrous result of it, are well known. It was reserved for the present Prince of Servia, Milosch Obrenovitch, to achieve the administrative independence of thé Principality.*

The Servian Pesmas, which are the work of centuries, and which, more than anything else perhaps, have served to keep alive in the people the sentiment of nationality, and to unite in a common animosity to the Turk all the kindred branches of the great Slave race in the East, may, all of them, be said to be lyrical, in so far as they are all of them made to be sung or recited to the *gouslé*, a rude musical instrument, with a single string, played on by a bow. But I have already observed that none of them possess those qualities which belong to what we now call lyric poetry. They may be classified under two heads, — the heroic pesmas, relating to

---

* Since these words were written, that extraordinary man has terminated a life perhaps unparalleled both in the duration and the activity of it. He is succeeded by his son, Prince Michael.

historical events and characters; and the domestic, or songs sung by the women, of an erotic or fantastio character. Of the former, I have given but a single specimen : that which relates to the battle of Kossovo, an event which was to the Serbs what the battle of Ceuta was to the Spaniards, of Hastings to the Saxons, and of Mohacs to the Magyars ; for I must avow that the greater number of these heroic *pesmas* abound in the description of atrocities which would be sickening to an English reader. They are, however (some of them), so deeply tinctured with a kind of terror unlike that suggested by any poetry which is known to me, that I greatly regret having been unable to reproduce them in some form which, whilst excluding revolting details, might have still preserved the inspiration of terror.

It is but a very few years since the poetry of the Serbs was first reduced to writing. I believe that M. Vouk Stefanovitch Karadjitch was the first to rescue these *pesmas* from that state of oral tradition in which they had existed for ages. Like the Greek rhapsodies, they are composed and sung about the land, from village to village, by blind beggars. The poets of Servia are the blind ; and surely there is something touching in this common consecration of the imaginary world as an hereditary possession to those from whose sense this visible world is darkened. The traveller, or the huntsman reposing from the chase, in some wild wayside *méhana* or tavern (a mere mud-cabin on the windy mountain-side, and generally near a mountain spring), as, followed by his dogs, he seats himself upon the bench by the ingle, may yet see, amid a group of eager, weather-beaten faces, the blind bard with his hollow wooden *gouslé*, covered with sheepskin, and traversed by a single string. This instrument is placed upon the knee, and played like a violoncello. First a series of long wailing notes commands the attention of the audience; then a pause, through which you hear the harsh grating of the *gouslé* string; and then forth roll the long monotonous verses of the pesma, of which Marko Kralievitch is probably the hero ; a sort of burly brawling Viking of the land, with just a touch in his composition of Roland and the Cid, but with much more about him of Gargantua.

I have already noticed the primitive simplicity of the Servian Pesmas. Amongst other causes, two chiefly have no doubt combined to preserve this in its original purity, — one, the mountain life, and the social isolation which has for centuries withdrawn the Serbs from the influence of any foreign history, religion, or mythology ;*  and the other, the fact

---

* It is indeed singular that, considering the relations once existing between Montenegro and the Republics of Venice and Ragusa, the national poetry of these mountaineers should have been so little influenced from abroad.

that the Turk, unlike European conquerors, has ever contented himself with superimposing on the conquered the authority of Islam, without any attempt to assimilate to himself the annexed population, either as regards language or legislation.

Another fact remains to be noticed in connection with the poetry of the Serbs. This is the almost entire absence of the mythic element. Nothing like the mysticism of the early Teutonic literature, the fairy fantasies of the Persian, or the weird cosmogony of the Scandinavian Eddas, is to be found in these *pesmas*. This, I suppose, must be attributed to the character of the Slavonic race. Neither is any trace to be found in their poetry of superstitions which are to this day dominant amongst the people themselves, such as the vampire and the witch. One striking exception, however, to this general rejection of the mystical exists in the frequent introduction of the *vila* as a supernatural agent. Here is, perhaps, the fragment of an unconjectured myth. These strange and solemn beings, whose vague and varying forms have not yet been defined, even by the imagination, — rarely seen, but often making heard, from the mountain and the wild, their voice of prophecy and of warning, — menacing and sometimes deadly to man when he invades their mighty solitudes, yet gifted with beneficent powers and healing arts, are they not, perhaps, symbols of forces, at once terrible and salutary in Nature, apparitions of her power, and echoes of her awful voice ?

Of the domestic *pesmas* I have given many specimens, and yet barely enough to indicate their vast variety. The sentiment of love as expressed in these songs is not (it will be remarked) that tender metaphysical motion of the soul which belongs to the North, and is perhaps the growth of a high civilization. It is rather a fierce, quick, meridional passion, the eager, instinctive, *mi piace* of the South, sensual but natural, and not without grace and delicacy.

What is most remarkable in these songs is their essentially dramatic character. Either they represent, in short close dialogue, a particular "situation," or they treat a particular phase of a particular sentiment or passion ; or else they relate in rapid narrative a particular event, commencing, without preamble, where the action commences, and terminating, without reflection or remark, where the action terminates. Another peculiarity is a certain playful slyness, which hardly amounts to humor, but is like the sport of an infant savage. They also abound in what appears, if I may say so, a sort of *naïve* cynicism, — the cynicism, not of embittered experience, but of childish incapacity for deep or earnest thought. The propensity to personify all things, and the familiar intercourse indicated in these *pesmas*, as existing between man and all nat-

ural objects, whether animate or inanimate, affords
obvious proof of those primitive conditions of soci-
ety to which I have already alluded.

The Servian metres are unrhymed, and trochaic
or dactylic in character. They consist of verses
varying from three to seventeen syllables in length.
Here is a specimen, —

Oblăk sě vīyě | pōvědrōm nēbŭ.

"The cloud floats in the pure ether."

It is an interesting and suggestive fact that the
natural quantity of the syllables is modified, in poetry, to suit the necessities of the metre. The following words, for instance, if pronounced without
reference to prosody, would be thus accentuated, —

I pōněsě | trī trōvěrǎ blāgǎ.

But when sung to the *gouslé* as a verse, they are to
be scanned thus, —

I pōněsě | trī trōvārǎ blāgǎ.

May not this throw a ray of light on the uneluci-
dated question of Greek accent and quantity?

But I have said enough. I will only add of the
contents of this little volume that, whether they be
weeds or wild-flowers, I have at least gathered them
on their native soil, amidst the solitudes of the Car-
pathians, and along the shores of the Danube.

OWEN MEREDITH.

# CONTENTS.

# HEROIC PESMA.

## THE BATTLE OF KOSSOVO.

### I.

THE Sultan Murad o'er Kossovo comes
With banners and drums.

There, all in characters fair,[1] *
He wrote a letter; and there
Bade his estaffettes despatch
To bear it to Krouchevatch,
To the white-walled town of the Tzar,
To the hands of Prince Lazar.

" Listen, Lazarus,[2] chief of the Serbs, to me!
That which never hath been, that which never
     shall be,

---

    * See Notes, pp. 51 – 54.

Is that two lords one land should sway,
And the same rayas two tributes pay.
Send to me, therefore, the tributes and keys;
The golden keys of each white town;
And send me a seven years' tribute with these.
But if this thou wilt not do,
Then come thou down over Kossovo:
On the field of Kossovo come thou down,
That we may divide the land with our swords.
These are my words."

When Lazarus this letter had read,
Bitter, bitter were the tears he shed.

## II.

A gray bird, a falcon, comes flying apace
From Jerusalem, from the Holy Place;
And he bears a light swallow abroad.
It is not a gray bird, a falcon, God wot!
But the Saint Elias; and it is not
A light swallow he bears from afar,
But a letter from the Mother of God
To the Tzar who in Kossovo stays.
And the letter is dropt on the knees of the
        Tzar,

And these are the words that it says : —
" Lazarus, Prince of a race that I love,
Which empire choosest thou ?
That of the heaven above ?
Or that of the earth below ?
If thou choose thee an earthly realm,
Saddle horse, belt, spur, and away !
Warriors, bind ye both sabre and helm,
And rush on the Turks, and they
With their army whole shall perish.
But, if rather a heavenly crown thou cherish,
At Kossovo build ye a temple fair.
There no foundations of marble lay,
But only silk of the scarlet dye.
Range ye the army in battle array,
And let each and all full solemnly
Partake of the blesséd sacrament there.
For then of a certainty know
Ye shall utterly perish, both thou
And thine army all ; and the Turk shall be
Lord of the land that is under thee."

When the Tzar he read these words,
His thoughts were as long and as sharp as
        swords.

" God of my fathers, what shall I choose ?
If a heavenly empire, then must I lose
All that is dearest to me upon earth ;
But if that the heavenly here I refuse,
What then is the earthly worth ?
It is but a day,
It passeth away,
And the glory of earth full soon is o'er,
And the glory of God is more and more."


" What is this world's renown ? "
(His heart was heavy, his soul was stirred.)
" Shall an earthly empire be preferred
To an everlasting crown ?
At Kossovo build me a temple fair :
Lay no foundations of marble down,
But only silk of the scarlet dye."
Then he sent for the Servian Patriarch :
With him twelve bishops to Kossovo went.
It was at the lifting of the dark :
They ranged the army in battle array,
And the army all full solemnly
Received the blessed sacrament,
And hardly was this done, when lo !
The Turks came rushing on Kossovo.

### III.

Ivan Kossantchitch, my pobratime,[3]
What of the Turk ?   How deem ye of him ?
Is he strong, is he many, is he near ?
Our battle, say ! may we show him ?
May we hope to overthrow him ?
What news of him bringest thou here ?


And Ivan Kossantchitch replied :
" Milosch Obìlitch, my brother dear,
I have lookt on the Turk in his pride.
He is strong, he is many, he is near,
His tents are on every side.
Were we all of us hewn into morsels, and
      salted,
Hardly, I think, should we salt him his meat.
Two whole days have I journeyed, nor halted,
Toward the Turk, near the Turk, round him,
      and never
Could I number his numbers, or measure his
      end.
From Eràble to Sazlia, brother, my feet
Have wandered ; from Sazlia round by the
      river,

Where the river comes round to the bridge
    with a bend;
And over the bridge to the town of Zvétchan;
From Zvétchan to Tchéchan, and farther, and
    ever
Farther, and over the mountains, wherever
Foot may fall, or eye may scan,
I saw naught but the Mussulman.

Eastward and westward, and southward and
    nor'ward,
Scaling the hillside, and scathing the gorse,
Horseman to horseman, and horse against
    horse
Lances like forests when forests are black;
Standards like clouds flying backward and for-
    ward,
White tents like snow-drifts piled up at the
    back.
The rain may, in torrents, fall down out of
    heaven,[4]
But never the earth will it reach:
Nothing but horsemen, nothing but horses,
Thick as the sands which the wild river courses
Leave, after tempest, in heaps on the beach.

Murad, for pasture, hath given
To his horsemen the plain of Mazguite.
Lances a-ripple all over the land,
Tost like the bearded and billowy wheat
By the winds of the mountain driven
Under the mountain slab.
Murad looks down in command
Over Sitnitza and Lab."


" Answer me, Ivan, answer ye me,
Where may the tent of Murad be ?
His milk-white tent, may one see it afar
O'er the plain, from the mountain, or out of
        the wood ?
For I have sworn to the Prince Lazar
A solemn vow upon Holy Rood,
To bring him the head of the Turkish Tzar,
And set my feet in his infidel blood.


" Art mad, my pobratime, art mad ?
Where may the tent be, the tent of Murad ?
In the midst of a million eyes and ears :
In the midst of a million swords and spears,
In the heart of the camp of the Turk.
Fatal thy vow is, and wild is the work ;

For hadst thou the wings of the falcon, to fly
Fleeter than lightning, along the deep sky,
The wings of the falcon, though fleet be they,
Would never bear thee thy body away."


And  Milosch  abjured  him :  "O  Ivan,  my
      brother
(Though not by the blood, yet more dear than
      all other),
See thou say nothing of this to our lord,
Lest  ye  sorrow  his  heart ;  and  say  never  a
      word,
Lest  our  friends  be  afflicted,  and  fail.    But
      thou
Shalt rather answer to who would know,
And boldly aver to the Tzar,
'The Turk is many, but more are we,
And easy and light is the victory :
For he is not an army of men of war,
But a rabble rather
Of rascals that gather
To the promise of plunder from places afar ;
Priests and pedlers,
Jugglers and fiddlers,
Dancers and drummers,

Varlets and mummers,
Boys and buffoons, — all craven loons
That never in burly of battle have bled,
Never have combated sword in hand ;
They are only come, the beggars, for bread,
And to feed on the fat of the land.
And the dreadful dismal dysentery
Is among their men, and their horses die
Of a daily increasing malady.' "


## IV.


Lazarus, lord of the Serbs, our Tzar,[5]
At Krouchevatch high Slava doth hold.
Around him, sitting by cups of gold,
His sons and his seigneurs are.


To right, the reverénd Youg Bogdan ;[6]
Round whom the nine young Yougovitch ;
To left, that thrice-accurséd man,
The traitor black, Vouk Brankovitch ;
And many a lord, along the board,
And last of all, in the knightly train,
Milosch, the manly Voïvod ;
Next him, Servian Voïvodes twain,

Ivan Kossantchitch, his brother in God,
And Milan Toplitza, a man without stain.

And the Tzar bade pour the purple wine,
And, brimming up his golden cup,
Lookt all adown that lordly line.

"To whom shall the King first pledge?" he
        began,
" If first to age, this health should be,
To no man do I drink but thee,
Revered old Youg Bogdan ;
But if to rank or high degree,
Vouk Brankovitch, I drink to thee.'
If to friendship be the toast,
My brothers nine, I know not which
Amongst you all I love the most,
You gallant-hearted Yougovitch !
If to beauty, then be thine,
Ivan, first the flowing wine.
If to length and strength of limb,
Then the wine to Milan brim,
No man measures height with him.
If to valor, more than even
Stature, beauty, friendship, age,

Our first honors should be given,
Then to Milosch must we pledge.
Yet, be that as it may be,
Milosch, I drink to none but thee!
Milosch, thy health!
Drink, man, drink!
Why should any man care to think?
Traitor or true, or friend or foe,
To thee I drain this goblet low;
And, ere to-morrow, at Kossovo,
Thou thy master hast betrayed
To the Turk, for wages paid,
(Friend or foe, whate'er befall,
True or traitor, what care I?)
The King drinks to thee in his hall,
Lip to lip, and eye to eye,
Pledge me now in sight of all;
And, since to thee I fill it up,
Take thou too this golden cup,
And add it to ill-gotten wealth, —
Milosch, thy health!"

Lightly Milosch bounded up,
Lightly caught the golden cup,
To the black earth bowed his head,

And, " Noble master, thanks ! " he said,
" For the pledge thou pledgest me,
And thanks that, of thy courtesy,
Thou to me dost first allot,
A true, true health, O King, to thee,
To pledge back in this golden token ;
Thanks for this, my lord, but not
For the words which thou hast spoken.
For, O, (and may my loyalty,
Dear liege, not fatal prove to me,
Before the truth is judged between
Us, and this fair company !)
My true heart is sound and clean,
Traitor never have I been,
Traitor never will I be !
But at Kossovo to-morrow morn
I trust, as I am a living man,
A soldier and a Christian,
To go to the death for the true, true faith,
True to the last where my faith is sworn,
Careless of calumny, scorning scorn !
The traitor is sitting by thy side,
He toucheth thy robe, thy wine he drinketh,
To God and his king he hath foully lied,
Vouk Brankovitch, the servile-eyed,

Christian false, and perjured friend!
God judge between us twain i' the end,
And perish he in the thought he thinketh!
To-morrow a noble day will be,
For at Kossovo all men shall see
What is the truth betwixt us two,
And who is traitor, and who is true.
For I swear by the great sun in the sky,
And I swear by the living God on high
That judgeth us all, whate'er befall,
When at Kossovo upon battle plain,
Murad, the Turk, I have sought and slain
(Sought and slain, for I swore by the rood
To set my feet in his Turkish blood),
If God but grant me safe and sane
A living man to come again
Back to white-walled Krouchevatch,
And there that traitor foul I catch,
Vouk Brankovitch, I will have by the throat.
All men shall see it, and all men shall note,
For it shall be done in the light of the sun.
To my good war-lance I will fix his skull,
As a woman fixes a ball of wool
To her distaff when her spinning is done.
Then I will bear him to Kossovo,

Bear him back to the battle plain;
All men shall see it, and all men shall know
Who is the traitor of us twain."


V.


At the royal board a noble pair
Sit together, and full sad they are.
Lazarus and his Militza fair,
The sweet-eyed Tzarina and the Tzar.
Troubled is the Tzar's broad brow,
The Tzarina's eyes are dim,
And, with tears that dare not flow,
The Tzarina says to him : —


"Lord Lazarus, O golden crown
Of Servia, and sweetheart my own!
To-morrow morn to Kossovo
With thee to the battle go
Servitors and Voïvodes.
I alone, in these abodes,
Vacant of thy voice, remain;
Hearing haply, on the wind,
Murmurs of the battle plain;
Heavy of heart, and sad of mind,

Silent in sorrow, alone with pain.
O think on this, my life, my lord,
Never a soul to carry a word
To Kossovo, from me to thee;
To Krouchevatch from thee to me;
Wherefore, lord, of my brothers nine,
The sons of Youg, our father old,
(Golden stars in a crown of gold!)
Let one, for once, be wholly mine.
Mine to witness the tears I weep;
Mine to solace the vigil I keep;
Mine alone, of my nine brothers,
To pray with me for those eight others;
Of brothers nine, but leave me one
To swear by when the rest be gone!" [8]

And Lazarus, lord of the Serbs, replied:
" Militza, sweetheart, wife true-eyed,
Of thy nine brothers, tell to me which
Thou lovest best, that he should rest
In our white palace to watch by thee.
Which of them, sweetheart? — tell to me!"
And she answered, " Bocko Yougovitch."

And Lazarus, lord of the Serbs, replied:
" Militza, sweetheart, wife true-eyed,

To-morrow, when from her red bower
The watery dawn begins to break,
Ere yet the sun hath felt his power,
Seek thou the city walls, and take
Thy post against the Eastern gate:
There shalt thou see the army pass,
To mantle the field in martial state,
And trample the dew-drop out of the grass.
All lusty warriors, leal and true,
Who in battle have never turned their backs,
In complete steel, with curtle axe;
Each spearman true, as his own true steel.
And, foremost of all, that, with iron heel,
Crush the wet violet down in the moss,
With purple plumes, in vesture rich,
Thy brother, Bocko Yougovitch,
Bearing the standard of the Cross.
Seize thou the golden bridle-ring,
Greet him fair from his lord the king,
And bid him that he the standard yield
To whomsoever he deemeth best,
And turn about from the battle-field,
In our white palace with thee to rest."

## VI.

Now, when the dawn from her red bower
Upclomb the chilly skies, and, all
Athwart the freshening city tower,
The silent light began to fall
About the breezy yellow flower
That shook on the shadowy city wall,
Militza, through the glimmering streets,
Goes forth against the Eastern gate.
There, all i' the morning light, she meets
The army on to the distant down,
Winding out of the dusky town,
To mantle the field in martial state,
And trample the dew-drop out of the grass.
O brothers, a goodly sight it was!
With curtle axe, in complete steel,
So many a warrior, lusty and leal,
So many a spearman, stout and true,
Marching to battle in order due.
And foremost among that stately throng,
With, over his helmet's golden boss,
Floating plumes of the purple rich
The gallant Bocko Yougovitch
Bearing the standard of the Cross.

All blazing gold his corselet beamed,
Imperial purple fold on fold,
The mighty Christian ensign streamed
Over his red-roan courser bold ;
And high upon the standard top
Against the merry morning gleamed
An apple wrought of purest gold ;
Thereon the great gold cross, from which,
All glittering downward, drop by drop,
Great golden acorns, lightly hung,
Over his shining shoulder flung
Flashes of light o'er Yougovitch.

She caught the bridle-ring : in check
The red-roan courser pawed the ground.
About her brother's bended neck
Her milk-white arm she softly wound,
And half in hope, and half in fear,
She whispered in the young man's ear :
" Brother, my liege and thine, the king,
Commits me to thy comforting.
He greets thee fair, and bids me say
(The which with all my heart I pray)
That thou the royal ensign yield
To whomsoever thou deemest best,

And turn about from the battle-field
At Krouchevatch with me to rest,
That of nine brothers I may have one
To swear by when the rest be gone."

But, " Foul befall," the young man said,
" The man that turns his horse's head,
Whoe'er he be, from battle plain :
Turn thee, sister, turn again
To thy white tower!   I will not yield
The Holy Cross 't is mine to bear,
Nor turn about from the battle-field.
Not, though the king should give, I swear,
The whole of Krouchevatch to me,
Would I turn thitherwards with thee.
To-day will be the noblest day
You sun in heaven did ever see ;
Nor shall my own true comrades say
This day, in sorrow or scorn, of me,
' The craven heart that dared not go
To the great fight at Kossovo ;
That feared to find a saintly death,
Nor poured his blood for Holy Rood,
Nor fell for the Christian faith.' "
He prickt his horse toward the gate,

And, through a cloud of hoary mist
Glittering like one great amethyst,
Swept forth into the morning wan.
Then up there rides in royal state,
With his seven sons, old Youg Bogdan.
She stopt them one by one ; she took
The bridle-rein ; she spoke to them all.
Not one of them all would turn and look :
Not one of them all would listen and wait ;
But the trumpet sounded in the gate,
And they followed the trumpet call.

And after these, a little space,
Voïn Yougovitch not far
She spied come riding at slow pace,
Leading the destriers of the Tzar,[9]
All trapt and housed with gold be they,
And going an amble by the way.
His good steed was of dapple gray.
She caught the bridle-ring : in check
The good gray courser pawed the ground.
Her milk-white arm she softly wound
About her brother's bended neck ;
And half in hope, and half in fear,
She whispered in the young man's ear :

"Brother, my liege and thine, the king,
Commits me to thy comforting.
He greets thee fair, and bids me say
(The which with all my heart I pray)
That thou the royal destriers yield
To whomsoever thou deemest best,
And turn about from the battle-field
In Krouchevatch with me to rest,
That of nine brothers I may have one
To swear by when the rest be gone."

But, " Sister, foul befall," he said,
" The man that turns his horse's head,
Whoe'er he be, from battle plain:
Turn thee, sister, turn again
To thy white tower!   I will not yield
The destriers of my lord the Tzar,
Nor turn about from the battle-field,
Where all my noble kinsmen are,
Albeit to meet my death I go
To the great fight at Kossovo;
To pour my blood for Holy Rood,
To fight to the death for the Christian faith,
With my kinsmen all to fight and fall,
With our foreheads against the foe."

Through the gate he prickt his steed,
And off to the dreary downs afar,
Leading as fast as he might lead
The destriers of the Tzar.
But Dame Militza, when no more
She heard the echoing hoofs that bore
Her brother from her, even as one
From whom the light of life is gone,
Fell swooning on the cold curbstone.

Then came the Tzar himself anon,
And his great war-horse, pacing on,
Did stoutly neigh in lusty pride;
But when he past beside that stone,
He stopt, and stoopt, and swerved aside.
There, all her fair white length o'erthrown,
The Tzar his own true wife espied,
And fast the bitter tears down ran,
As he called to his servant, Gouloban:
" Good Gouloban, my faithful friend,
In this thy trusty service prove;
From off thy milk-white horse descend,
And, as thou dost thy master love,
In thy true arms thy mistress take,
With whom to her tall tower go;

And, God forgive thee for my sake,
But go not thou to Kossovo.
I will requite thee when again
I meet thee, if I be not slain :
Howbeit, I deem my doom at hand,
For the Turk is lord of half the land."

Down stept the trusty serving-man,
Full fast his bitter tears down ran,
And sad was the heart of Gouloban.
He lifted up that drooping flower,
Lifted her on to his milk-white steed,
And rode with her to her tall tower,
As fast as he might speed.

There laid he her in linen bed,
And lowly laid her lovely head.
But o'er the airy morning smote,
Along the blowing breeze remote,
A solitary trumpet-note.
Full well the milk-white war-horse knew
The music of that martial sound,
And in the courtyard pawed the ground,
And blithely from his nostrils blew
The morning mist.   Then Gouloban

Adown the turret stairway ran,
He leapt to stirrup, he leapt to selle.
From fleeting hands he waved farewell;
Again he heard the trumpet blow,
And he rode back to Kossovo.

## VII.

All when the misty morn was low,
And the rain was raining heavily,
Two ravens came from Kossovo,
Flying along a lurid sky: [10]
One after one, they perched upon
The palace of the great Lazar,
And sat upon the turret wall.
One 'gan croak, and one 'gan call,
" Is this the palace of the Tzar?
And is there never a soul inside? "

Was never a soul within the hall,
To answer to the ravens' call,
Save Militza.   She espied
The two black birds on the turret wall,
That all in the wind and rain did croak,
And thus the ravens she bespoke :

" In God's great name, black ravens, say,
Whence came ye on the wind to-day?
Is it from the plain of Kossovo?
Hath the bloody battle broke?
Saw ye the two armies there?
Have they met? And, friend or foe,
Which hath vanquisht? How do they fare?"

And the two black fowls replied:
" In God's great name, Militza, dame,
From Kossovo at dawn we came.
A bloody battle we espied:
We saw the two great armies there,
They have met, and ill they fare.
Fallen, fallen, fallen are
The Turkish and the Christian Tzar.
Of the Turks is nothing left;
Of the Serbs a remnant rests,
Hackt and hewn, carved and cleft,
Broken shields, and bloody breasts."
And lo! while yet the ravens spoke,
Up came the servant, Miloutine:
And he held his right hand, cleft
By a ghastly sabre stroke,
Bruised and bloody, in his left;

Gasht with gashes seventeen
Yawned his body where he stood,
And his horse was dripping blood.

" O sorrow, sorrow, bitter woe
And sorrow, Miloutine ! " she said ;
" For now I know my lord is dead.
For, were he living; well I know,
Thou hadst not left at Kossovo
Thy lord forsaken to the foe."

And Miloutine spake, breathing hard :
" Get me from horse : on cool greensward
Lay me, lay me, mistress mine :
A little water from the well
To bathe my wounds in water cold,
For they are deep and manifold ;
And touch my lip with rosy wine,
That I may speak before I die.
I would not die before I tell
The tale of how they fought and fell."
She got him from his bloody steed,
And wiped the death-drops from his brow,
And in the fresh grass laid him low ;
And washt his wounds in water cold,

For they were deep and manifold ;
Full ghastly did they gape and bleed :
She stanched them with her garment's fold,
And lightly held his body up,
And bathed his lips with rosy wine,
And all the while her tears down ran,
And dropt into the golden cup ;
And still she questioned of the war :

"O tell me, tell me, Miloutine,
Where fell the glorious Prince Lazar ?
Where are fallen my brothers nine ?
Where my father, Youg Bogdan ?
Where Milosch, where Vouk Brankovitch ?
And where Strahinia Banovitch ?

Then when the servant, Miloutine,
Three draughts had drained of rosy wine,
Although his eyes were waxing dim,
A little strength came back to him.
He stood up on his feet, and, pale
And ghastly, thus began the tale :

"They will never return again,
Never return ! ye shall see them no more ;

Nor ever meet them within the door,
Nor hold their hands. Their hands are
    cold,
Their bodies bleach in bloody mould.
They are slain ! all of them slain !
And the maidens shall mourn, and the mothers
    deplore,
Heaps of dead heroes on battle plain.
Where they fell, there they remain,
Corpses stiff in their gore.
But their glory shall never grow old.
Fallen, fallen, in mighty war,
Fallen, fighting about the Tzar,
Fallen, where fell our lord Lazar !
Never more be there voice of cheer !
Never more be there song or dance !
Muffled be moon and star !
For broken now is the lance,
Shivered both shield and spear,
And shattered the scimitar.
And cleft is the golden crown,
And the sun of Servia is down,
O'erthrown, o'erthrown, o'erthrown,
The roof and top of our renown,
Dead is the great Lazar !

"Have ye seen when the howling storm-wind
    takes
The topmost pine on a hoary rock,
Tugs at it, and tears, and shakes, and breaks,
And tumbles it into the ocean ?
So when this bloody day began, —
In the roaring battle's opening shock,
Down went the gray-haired Youg Bogdan.
And following him, the noblest man
That ever wore the silver crown
Of age, grown gray in old renown.
One after one, and side by side
Fighting, thy nine brothers died :
Each by other, brother brother
Following, till death took them all.
But of these nine the last to fall
Was Bocko.   Him, myself, I saw,
Three awful hours — a sight of awe,
Here, and there, and everywhere,
And all at once, made manifest,
Like a wild meteor in a troubled air,
Whose motion never may be guest.
For over all the lurid rack
Of smoking battle, blazed and burned,
And streamed and flasht,

Like flame before the wind upturned
The great imperial ensign splasht
With blood of Turks: where'er he dasht
Amongst their bruised battalions, I
Saw them before him reel and fly:
As when a falcon from on high,
Pounce on a settle-down of doves,
That murmurs make in myrrhy groves,
Comes flying all across the sky,
And scatters them with instant fright;
So flew the Turks to left and right,
Broken before him.   Milosch fell,
Pursued by myriads down the dell,
Upon Sitnitza's rushy brink,
Whose chilly waves will roll, I think,
So long as time itself doth roll,
Red with remorse that they roll o'er him.
Christ have mercy on his soul,
And blesséd be the womb that bore him.
Not alone he fell.   Before him
Twelve thousand Turkish soldiers fell,
Slaughtered in the savage dell.
His right hand was wet and red
With the blood that he had shed,
And in that red right hand he had

(Shorn from the shoulder sharp) the head
Of the Turkish Tzar, Murad.


" There resteth to Servia a glory,
A glory that shall not grow old ;
There remaineth to Servia a story,
A tale to be chanted and told !
They are gone to their graves grim and gory,
The beautiful, brave, and bold ;
But out of the darkness and desolation,
Of the mourning heart of a widowed nation,
Their memory waketh an exultation !
Yea, so long as a babe shall be born,
Or there resteth a man in the land —
So long as a blade of corn
Shall be reapt by a human hand —
So long as the grass shall grow
On the mighty plain of Kossovo —
So long, so long, even so,
Shall the glory of those remain
Who this day in battle were slain.


" And as for what ye inquire
Of Vouk, — when the worm and mole
Are at work on his bones, may his soul

Eternally singe in hell-fire !
Curst be the womb that bore him !
Curst be his father before him !
Curst be the race and the name of him !
And foul as his sin be the fame of him !
For blacker traitor never drew sword —
False to his faith, to his land, to his lord !
And doubt ye, doubt ye, the tale I tell ?
Ask of the dead, for the dead know well ;
Let them answer ye, each from his mouldy bed,
For there is no falsehood among the dead :
And there be twelve thousand dead men know
Who betrayed the Tzar at Kossovo."

# NOTES.

## NOTE 1, page 19.

The word is *sitni*, " fine, slender, elaborate." This, in Servian poetry, is the epithet invariably applied to hand-writing; and the deference and wonder with which the writing of a letter, or the use of pen, ink, and paper, in any shape, is alluded to throughout the poetry of the Serbs, sufficiently indicates an elementary and barbarous condition of social life.

## NOTE 2, page 19.

Lazarus Grebleanovitch is sometimes called Tzar, some-times knès or prince. But he was consecrated Tzar in 1376.

## NOTE 3, page 23.

The word *Pobratime* (from *brat*, "brother") denotes a re-lationship (independent of blood or kindred) between per-sons of the same sex, which is peculiar to the Serbs. For in the Bulgarian the word signifies nothing more than friend. But in Servia it constitutes a relationship volunta-rily contracted, but so close as to be incompatible with mar-riage between the one Pobratime and the sister of the other (*see* note to page 97). In the ancient Servian liturgies are to be found prayers applicable to the consecration of this relationship by the priest. It is a sort of freemasonry, and obliges those who have contracted it to succor each other in danger or sickness. Appeal in such cases, the usual form of which it is held impious to reject, and which, in the Serb poetry, is sometimes placed in the mouth even of Turks and Vilas, is "*Bogom bratá* (or *sestra*) *i soetim Jovanom*," "My brother, or sister, in God and Saint John."

### NOTE 4, page 24.

The whole of this passage is quite Oriental in the hyperbolical character of the similes it piles together. Strange, that Marlowe, in (perhaps his greatest) play of "Tamburlaine," should have placed in the mouth of an Oriental monarch very similar language :

(*King of Morocco,* loquitur :)
" *The spring is hindered by your smothering host;*
*For neither rain can fall upon the earth,*
*Nor sun reflex his virtuous beams thereon,*
*The ground is mantled with such multitudes.*"

Was it by intuition ? But Marlowe himself rivals the Orientals in gigantesque exaggeration and supercilious indifference to simplicity.

### NOTE 5, page 27.

The *slava* (literally "glory") is a very ancient custom peculiar to the Serbs, and still honored in the observance. Every family, or tribe (rather in the sense of the Roman *gens*), independently of the patron saints particular to each of its individual members, has a patron common to them all, as Saint Dimitri, Saint Nicholas, Saint Elias, etc. ; who is, on periodical occasions, celebrated with certain ceremonies of a convivial kind, beginning in solemn libation to some sacred toast, and ending in general intoxication. These ceremonies are called *slaviti slavou,* and the toasts *zradavita.* It is the popular belief that the celebrated Servian hero,

Marko Kralievitch, annually returns to life on the 5th of May, and holds, in the church of Prilip, the Slava of St. George.

## Note 6, page 27.

All these personages are historical, and figure in the Pesmas which refer to the great battle of Kossovo. Youg Bogdan (*youg*, " South ") was the father-in-law of Lazarus, and Governor of Acarnania and Macedonia. Yougovitch, the sons of Youg — *vitch*, or *vitz*, always implying " son of " — as Alexander Karageorgiovitz, son of Kara-George ; Milosch Obrenovitz, son of Obren, the last and present Prince of Servia.

## Note 7, page 28.

Vouk Brankovitch, a son-in-law of Lazarus. A circumstance similar to that which forms the main plot of the Niebelungen, namely, a quarrel between the wives of the two men, is supposed to have led to that deadly hatred between Vouk and Milosch Obilitch, which ultimately brought about the defection of the one and the death of the other. Of the estimation in which the memory of this personage is held amongst the Serbs and other Sclavic races, judge from the following passage in the Code of Montenegro, dated 1803 :

" And if, from this day henceforth, any Montenegrin should be found capable of betraying his country, we devote him, beforehand, to the eternal malediction reserved for Judas, who betrayed the Lord God, and the infamous Vouk Brankovitch, who betrayed the Serbs at Kossovo, and thus forfeited the divine mercy."

## Note 8, page 33.

The affection between brother and sister, or brother and brother, would appear to be held among the Serbs as more sacred than that arising out of any other relationship. Ironical comparison frequently occurs throughout the Servian poetry between the affection of wife to husband, and of sister to brother, not to the advantage of the former. Consequently the oath sworn "by a brother" is especially sacred, and not to have "a brother to swear by" is held to be a family disgrace. The whole poem of "Predag and Nenad" (which I have not translated) is founded on this sense of humiliation, involved in the fact of not having a brother to swear by.

NOTE 9, page 38.

For the use of this word, destriers, I plead the authority of Chaucer.

" And, for he was a knight auntrous.
He n'oldë sleepen in none hous,
But liggen in his hood,
His brightë helm was his avenger,
And by him baited his destrer,
Of herbës fine and good."

*Rime of Sir Thopas.*

NOTE 10, page 42.

In the Servian poetry, ravens are the invariable bearers of ill tidings.

# POPULAR OR DOMESTIC PESMAS.

## THE STAG AND THE VILA.

'ER the mountain the wild stag browses
the mountain herbage alone,
At morn he browses, at noon he sick-
ens, at eve he maketh moan.
From the rifts of the rocky quarries the Vila *
hears him, and calls,

---

\* The Vilas are supernatural beings that appear frequently in the poetry, and exist to this day in the popular superstition, of the Serbs. I have been unable to trace their origin, but they would seem to be a remnant of the early Slave mythology; and, being a mountain race, to have survived the fate of the lowland members of the fairy family, notwithstanding the presence of perhaps almost as many "holy freres" as those to whose "*blessing of thorpes and dairies*," Chaucer, in his day, attributed the fact that "*there bin no faëries.*" They are a kind of fierce Oreads, dwelling among the mountains and forests, and sometimes about the margin of waste waters. Their attributes are varying, and not distinctly ascertainable, but they are mostly terrible, and hos-

" O beast of the mountain meadows, the woods,
and the waterfalls,
What sorrow is thine, so great that, browsing
at morn, at noon thou ailest,
And now to the stars thou art moaning? What
is it that thou bewailest ? "
And the stag to the Vila makes answer, mournfully moaning low :

---

tile to man. They are not, however, incapable of sympathy
with the human race; for they have been known (though
generally after being vanquished by them) to love great
heroes. Evidence of this is to be found in the recorded ex-
ploits of Marko Kralievitch. That hero was beloved by one
of these beings, who, indeed, prophesied his death, and that
of his horse, Charatz. This animal was aged above one hundred and fifty years at the period of his death, and, accord-
ing to some authorities, was the gift of a Vila. The love of
these beings, however, is generally treacherous, and often
fatal. The Vilas are not immortal, nor invulnerable. The
Vila Ravioela, who wounded the voïvode Milosch with a
golden arrow, was nearly massacred by Marko. They preserve, however, through incalculable time, supernatural
youth and beauty. They believe in God and Saint John, and
abhor the Turks. When they appear to mortal eyes it is as

"Unwedded maids,
Shadowing more beauty in their airy brows
Than have the white breasts of the Queen of Love,"

with long hair floating over their shoulders, and clothed in
snow-white vesture. They are wise in the use of herbs and
simples, they know the properties of every flower and berry,
and possess strange medical arts.

" O queen of the mountain, my sister ! I mourn
    for my lost white doe,
My milk-white doe, my darling ! from me, o'er
    the mountain track,
She wandered away to the fountain ; she wan-
    dered, she never came back.
Either forlornly she wanders, mourning me,
    missing her way,
Or the hunters have followed and found her,
    and she hath perisht their prey,
Or else she forgets me, the faithless thing ! and
    ever by valley and crag
Strays wanton after a belling note, and follows
    another stag.
If she be lost in the lonesome places, and hol-
    lows under the moon,
I pray that God, of his goodness, will guide her
    back to me soon.
If the hunters have slain my beloved one, wan-
    dering the woodland alone,
I pray that God, of his justice, will send them
    a fate like my own ;
But if she follows another stag, caring no more
    to come back,
I pray that God, in his vengeance, guide the
    hunter fleet on her track."

## LOVE AND SLEEP.

WALKT the high and hollow wood,
 from dawn to even-dew,
The wild-eyed wood stared on me,
 and unclaspt, and let me through,
Where mountain pines, like great black birds,
 stood percht against the blue.

Not a whisper heaved the woven woof of those
 warm trees :
All the little leaves lay flat, unmoved of bird
 or breeze :
Day was losing light all round, by indolent de-
 grees.

Underneath the brooding branches, all in holy
 shade,
Unseen hands of mountain things a mossy
 couch had made :
There asleep among pale flowers my beloved
 was laid.

Slipping down, a sunbeam bathed her brows
    with bounteous gold,
Unmoved upon her maiden breast her heavy
    hair was rolled,
Her smile was silent as the smile on corpses
    three hours old.

"O God!" I thought, "if this be death, that
    makes not sound nor stir!"
My heart stood still with tender awe, I dared
    not waken her,
But to the dear God, in the sky, this prayer I
    did prefer :

" Grant, dear Lord, in the blesséd sky, a warm
    wind from the sea,
To shake a leaf down on my love from yonder
    leafy tree ;
That she may open her sweet eyes, and haply
    look on me."

The dear God, from the distant sea, a little
    wind release,
It shook a leaflet from the tree, and laid it on
    her breast.
Her sweet eyes oped, and looked on me.
    How can I tell the rest ?

## TITTLE-TATTLE.

WO lovers kist in the meadow green,
They thought there was none to espy:
But the meadow green told what it
    had seen
To the white flock wandering by.
The white flock told it the shepherd:
The shepherd the traveller from far:
The traveller told it the mariner,
Watching the pilot star:
The mariner told it his little bark:
The little bark told it the sea:
The sea told it the river,
Flowing down by the lea:
The river told it the maiden's mother,
And so to the maid it came back:
The maiden, as soon as she heard it,
Curst them all for a tell-tale pack:
" Meadow, be barren forever,
Grass, grow not henceforth from the mould of
    thee !
Flock, be devoured by the wolf!

Shepherd, the Turk seize hold of thee!
Traveller, rot of the fever!
Mariner, drown in the gulf!
Bark, may the whirlwind perplex thee,
And break thee against the shore!
Sea, may the moon ever vex thee!
River, be dry evermore!"

## MATRIMONIAL CONSIDERATIONS.

HERE mountains shut the silence up,
    a milk-white maiden stood;
Her face was like a light, and kindled
    all the solitude.
And, while the wild white mountain flowers
    turned passionately pale,
And while the chilly water ran reluctant to the
    vale,
And the bald eagle, near the sun, stood still on
    some tall peak,
That milk-white maiden to her own sweet face
    began to speak:

" O face, sweet source of all my care,
Fair face (because I know thee fair!)

If I knew thou shouldst be kist
By any husband, withered, old, and gray,
I would wander, mist-like, with the mist,
The monstrous mountain many a league away,
Until, in some abandoned place,
Where the starved wolf cracks the bones
Of perisht men, and the wind groans
For want of something to devour,
I should find, wild in the wind,
Among the blotcht and mildewed stones,
The harsh-blowing absinthe flower;
And pluck the stubborn root of it,
That from the bitter fruit of it
I might the blighting juice express;
Therewith to bathe thee, O my face, my face!
Till all thy beauty should be bitterness,
And each unloved caress
Burn on the old man's lip, which should em-
         brace
Death on thy rosy portals, O my face!


"But if I knew, O my face, my face!
That thy lips should be kist by whom I would
         list,
I would glide, unespied, to a place, my face,

Where red roses, I know, ripely ripple and
blow,
And white lilies grow more snowy than snow;
And all in the balmy evening light,
While the dew is new, and the stars but a
few,
The roses so red, and the lilies so white,
I would pluck, with the sunset upon them, and
press
From those flowers their sweetest sweetnesses,
To embalm thee, my face, till what he should
embrace
Should be fairer than lilies and richer than
roses;
So that when on thy lips my beloved one re-
poses,
A thousand summers of fragrant sighs
Might fan the faint fire of his soul's desire
With raptures pure as the rivers that rise
Among the valleys of Paradise."

## LOVE CONFERS NOBILITY.

### HE.

IOLET,* little one mine!
  I would love thee, but thou art so
    small.

### SHE.

Love me, my love, from those heights of thine,
And I shall grow tall, so tall!
The pearl is small, but it hangs above
A royal brow, and a kingly mind:
The quail is little, little my love,
But she leaves the hunter behind.

---

* Violet is a pet name, as well as a proper name.

.

## A SOUL'S SWEETNESS.

### HE.

MAIDEN of my soul !
  What odor from the orange hast thou
    stole,
That breathes about thy breast with such sweet
    power ?
What sweetness, unto me
More sweet than amber honey to the bee
That builds i' the oaken bole,
And sucks the essential summer of the year
To store with sweetest sweets her hollow
    tower ?
Or is it breath of basil, maiden dear ?
Or of the immortal flower ?

### SHE.

By the sweet heavens, young lover !
No odor from the orange have I stole ;
Nor have I robbed for thee,
Dearest, the amber dower
Of the building bee,

From any hollow tower
In oaken bole :
But if, on this poor breast thou dost discover
Fragrance of such sweet power,
Trust me, O my belovéd and my lover,
'T is not of basil, nor the immortal flower,
But from a virgin soul.

## REMINISCENCES.

### HE.

AND art thou wed, my Belovéd?
My Belovéd of long ago!

### SHE. ·

I am wed, my Belovéd.   And I have given
A child to this world of woe.
And the name I have given my child is thine :
So that, when I call to me my little one,
The heaviness of this heart of mine
For a little while may be gone.
For I say not . . . "Hither, hither, my son ! "
But . . . "Hither, my Love, my Belovéd ! "

## SLEEP AND DEATH.

THE morning is growing: the cocks
are crowing:
Let me away, love, away!

'T is not the morning light;
Only the moonbeam white.
Stay, my white lamb, stay,
And sleep on my bosom, sleep!

The breeze is blowing: the cattle are lowing.
Let me away, love, away!

'T is not the cattle there;
Only the call to prayer.
Stay, my white lamb, stay,
And sleep on my bosom, sleep!

The Turks are warning to the mosk: 't is
morning:
Let me away, love, away!

'T is not the Turks, sweet soul!
Only the wolves that howl.
Stay, my white lamb, stay,
And sleep on my bosom, sleep!

The white roofs are gleaming : the glad chil-
    dren screaming :
Let me away, love, away!

'T is the night-clouds that gleam :
The night-winds that scream.
Stay, my white lamb, stay,
And sleep on my bosom, sleep!

My mother in the gateway calls to me: "Come
    straightway!"
And I must away, love, away!

Thy mother's in her bed,
Dumb, holy, and dead.
Stay, my white lamb, stay,
And sleep on my bosom, sleep!

## A CONJUGAL DISPUTE.

LL at the mid of the night, there arose
A quarrel 'twixt husband and wife ;
For, the young Omer Bey and his
    spouse,
Falling into discussion and strife,
Wild words to each other they said,
Side by side, at the dead
Of the night, on their marriage bed.
Had it been about anything less
The quarrel might have past by ;
But it was not a trifle, you guess,
That set words running so high.
Yet the cause in dispute (to be brief)
Was only a white handkerchief,
Broidered all over with gold,
And scented with rose and with amber,
So sweet the whole house could not hold
That scent from the nuptial chamber.
For (the whole truth herewith to disclose),
This handkerchief bordered with gold,
And scented with amber and rose,

Had been given to the Bey (to enfold
Her letters, which lay on his breast),
By the mistress that he loved best.
But his wife had a sensitive nose
For the scent of amber and rose ;
And the fiend himself only knows
Whether, but for a lie, ere the close
Of that quarrel there had not been blows.

" You know I 've a sister, my treasure,
The wife of our friend Zekir Bey ;
I love her, you know, beyond measure,
And she, dear, on our bridal day,
To me gave this white handkerchief,
Broidered all over with gold,
And scented with amber and rose ;
Which precious, for her sake, I hold,
Though the scent of it, much to my grief,
Has troubled our nuptial repose."

Smiling, her husband she heard,
Feeling no faith in his word,
For troubled his face was, she saw.
Up she leapt by the light of the taper,
Barefooted, and seized ink and paper ;
And wrote to her sister-in-law :

" Wife of our friend, Zekir Bey,
Long live thy husband, naught ail him,
Mayst thou never have cause to bewail him!
Speak truth, and fear nothing.   But say
(For truly the truth must be told)
To thy brother, on our bridal day,
Didst thou give a white handkerchief, brightly
Embroidered all over with gold,
And scented with rose and with amber
So sweet, that the scent of it nightly
May be smelt in the Bey's bridal chamber ? "

When this came to the wife of the Bey,
She burst into tears, as she read :
And " Pity upon me ! " she said,
" For I know not, alas ! what to say.
If I speak truth, I put strife
'Twixt the brother I love and his wife ;
If I speak false, much I dread
Lest my husband die for it," she said.

Then the letter she laid in her breast,
And she pondered with many a sigh,
" I choose of two evils the least,
If my husband must die, let him die !

Since the choice lies 'twixt one or the other, —
Any husband a woman may spare,
But the sister that injures a brother
Does that which she cannot repair."

Thus shrewdly the matter she saw:
And she wrote to her sister-in-law:

" Wife of my brother, the Bey !
My husband is well.   May naught ail him !
And I trust I shall never bewail him.
To my brother on your marriage day
(And truly the truth shall be told)
I gave a white handkerchief brightly
Embroidered all over with gold,
And scented with rose and with amber
So sweet, that the scent (as you say,
And as I cannot doubt of it) nightly
May be smelt in the Bey's bridal chamber."

## DEGREES OF AFFECTION.

UP and down the Tchardak,* underneath the blossomed roof,
 Musing, young Iövo,† at midnoon,
  walkt all aloof.
Suddenly the Tchardak broke beneath him :
 slipping through
The rotten plank, he fell, and his right arm was
 snapt in two.
Straight, a leech he sought him. Evil leech,
 in truth, he found.
Save the mountain Vila, none had skill to heal
 the wound :
But the Vila claimed in price of service, ere
 the cure began,
The right hand of the mother of the maimed
 and mangled man ;
The long hair of his sister with the riband in
 the hair ;

---

 * A sort of gallery or veranda, running round a house.
Also, sometimes, a pavilion, summer-house, or granary.
 † Diminutive for Iovan or John.

And the white pearl necklace which his wife
     was wont to wear.
The mother gave her right hand, and the sister
     gave her curls;
But the wife refused her necklace ... "I? I
     will not give my pearls!
Each is perfect, each is precious, nowhere else
     is such a set.
'T was my dowry from my father, and I mean
     to wear it yet."
This the Vila of the mountain heard; and,
     angered in her mood,
She dropt a little purple drop of poison in the
     food
Of young Iövo, and he died.

               Then, for the murdered man,
Those three women to lament, in funeral dole
     began.
One there was that, deeply mourning, ever-
     more did grieve:
One that missed and mourned for him at morn-
     ing and at eve:
One that mourned him now and then, with
     eyes a little dim,

And looks a little changed, whenever she re-
    membered him.
She whose sorrow ceased not, mourning more
    than any other,
Missing aye her murdered son, was young
    Iövo's mother:
She that mourned at morning, and at evening
    mourned, and missed her
Brother, when day came or went, was young
    Iövo's sister.
She that mourned him now and then, when
    sometimes in her life
Old memories filled vacant hours, was young
    Iövo's wife.

## THE FAIR IKONIA.

HE fair Ikonia boasted at the bath,
    Gayly, amidst the matrons ... " Tell
      me which
Amongst you, matrons, such a husband hath
As mine, Iövo Morniakovitch?
Where he goeth, there I go:

Where he resteth, there rest I :
Is he silent, then I know
That he names me silently:
Does he speak? of me he speaketh:
Does he dream? of me he dreameth :
Does he wake? for me he waketh :
Mine by night, when moonlight beameth !
Mine at dawn, when daylight breaketh ?
First from dreams of me to wake,
That his kiss may ope my eyes :
*'Dear, the dawn begins to break,*
*Light of my life, arise ! arise !'*
Life is long, the journey through it
Lone and weary, others tell.
I shall never turn and miss him
From my side, and this is well."
This the wily widow, Anna,
Heard, and slyly slipt away :
Then she clothed herself with splendor
And she stood, in rich array,
Where, from the Bazar, Iövo
Came home, singing all the way :
Deckt her cheeks with painted roses,
Darker dyed her midnight hair,
Breathed the breath of perfumed posies,

Laid her bounteous bosom bare,
Stood like glory in the gateway,
Murmured, mild as evening air,
"Sad, Iövo, seems thy case,
Wedded to a barren wife ;
If thou wouldst not see thy race
Pass and perish with thy life,
Wed with me, and I will bear thee
Every year a noble heir,
Every year a gracious infant,
With strong hands and golden hair." *


Long he listened : soft her voice was ;
Long he lookt : her dark eyes glistened.
As the counsel, so the choice was.
All too long he lookt and listened.
Thus the wily widow, Anna,
Won Iövo then and there :
And each year a boy she bore him
With strong hands and golden hair.
Silent walkt the fair Ikonia,

---

* The epithet "golden" generally implies "strength" in the Serb poetry. The words are literally "with golden hands," etc.

Making neither moan nor word,
Up the great Bazar walkt silent,
And she bought herself a cord :

In the garden square a golden
Orange-tree grows all alone,
There her silken cord she fastened,
And she hanged herself thereon.

Came one running to Iövo,
" On thy golden orange-tree,
Fair Ikonia, dead, is hanging."

" Hanging ?  Let her hang ! " quoth he,
" I 've a fairer far than she."

## A WISH.

WOULD I were a rivulet,
And I know where I would run !
To Save, the chilly river,
Where the market boats pass on ;
To see my dear one stand

By the rudder; and whether the rose
Which, at parting, I put in his hand,
Warm with a kiss in it, blows;
Whether it blows or withers:
I pluckt it on Saturday;
I gave it to him on Sunday;
On Monday he went away.

## IMPERFECTION.

ALL in the spring,
 When little birds sing,
  And flowers do talk
From stalk to stalk;
Whispering to a silver shower,
A violet did boast to be
Of every flower the fairest flower
That blows by lawn or lea.
But a rose that blew thereby
Answered her reproachfully
(All in the spring,
When little birds sing,
And flowers do talk

From stalk to stalk) :
"Violet, I marvel me
Of fairest flowers by lawn or lea
The fairest thou shouldst boast to be;
For one small defect I spy,
Should make thee speak more modestly :
Thy face is fashioned tenderly,
But then it hangs awry."


## EMANCIPATION.

HE Day of Saint George ! and a girl
prayed thus :
"O Day of Saint George, when again
to us
Thou returnest, and they carouse
Here in my mother's house,
Mayst thou find me either a corpse or a bride,
Either buried or wed ;
Rather married than dead ;
But however that may betide,
And whether a corpse or a spouse,
No more in my mother's house."

## THE VOICE OF NATURE ; OR, WHAT THE FISH SAID TO THE MAIDEN.

Y the sea a maiden is sitting,
 And she says to herself at her knit-
  ting :

" O my heart ! what more deep than the ocean,
Or more wide than the plain, can be ?
Or more swift than the horse in his motion ?
Or more sweet than the food of the bee ?
Or more dear than a brother ? "

And a fish from the sea replies :

"O maiden, but little wise !
The plain is less wide than the sea,
And the heaven more deep than this is ;
Eyes swifter than horses be ;
And honey less sweet than kisses ;
And a lover more dear than all other."

## THE MALADY OF MOÏO.

OÏO, the Tzarovitch (bolder is no
man ! )
Walkt to the Bath with the Turk
lords one day :
Mahmoud the Pacha's white wife (and what
woman
Is fairer than she is ?) was walking away.
Even as the sun, o'er the ardors of even,
Looks on the moon, and the moon on the sun,
Wistfully, each, disunited in heaven,
Soon to be pacing far pathways alone,
So through the mist of a moment of ecstasy,
Thrilled with a rapture delicious and dim,
Mute on the pale Pachinitza the Tzarovitch
Gazed, and the pale Pachinitza on him.
Moïo walkt silently back to his palace :
Troubled his heart was, and changed was his
mood.
Straightway he sickened of love, and lay dying,
Dying of love for the wife of Mahmoud.
Ladies the loveliest all came to visit him :

Only the wife of Mahmoud stayed away.
Then the Sultana rose up and wrote to her:
" Wouldst thou be greater than all of us, say?
Moïo is lying upon his couch dying;
Sore is his sickness, and fatal, they say :
Ladies the loveliest all come to visit him,
Thou, art thou more, Pachinitza, than they ? "
She, when she heard of it, loopt up her white
      sleeve,
Loopt up her light robe as white as a star ;
Presents she bore for him, worthy a monarch's
      son,
Figs from the sea-coast, and grapes from Mos-
      tar.
Lightly she trod o'er the long golden gallery,
Past all ungreeted the corridor dim,
Pale, the dumb purple pavilion she entered,
Where the Sultana was watching by him.
Softly she sat by his bedside, and softly
Wiped from his forehead the fever, and said,
" This is a malady known to me surely !
Long did I watch, and long weep by the bed
Once where my brother lay moaning and mad
      of it,
Moaning and maddened, unable to move;

Poison they said it was.   I, too, have drunk
> of it.
This is the passionate poison of love."
Trembling he listened, as trembling she ut-
> tered it.
Lightly he leapt from the couch where he lay,
Fastened, behind her, the long golden gallery,
Laught as he sank on her soft lips, and they
Three white days, little heeding the daylight,
Three blue nights, little noting the moon,
Sealed by sweet kisses in silent caresses,
Rested, while round them May melted to June.
Gayly the nightingale sang in the garden.
Love the bird sang of, and sweet was the tune.
Three white days, little loving the daylight,
Three blue nights, ill at rest 'neath the moon,
Mahmoud the Pacha walkt, mourning his
> miss'd one,
"Come, Pachinitza, come back to me soon!"
Sadly the nightingale sang in his garden.
Love the bird sang of, but harsh was the tune.
Then, when the fourth day was low in the
> orient,
Mahmoud the Pacha sat down in his hall ;
There a white letter he wrote to the Sultan :

"Sultan Imperial, dear master of all!
There's a white dove, with a gold treasure
    casket,
Flown to thy doors from thy servant's abode.
Send back my white dove, restore me my
    treasure,
If thou hast fear of the justice of God."
But to the Pacha the Sultan sent answer:
"Mahmoud, my servant, behoves thee to know
There's in my palace a falcon unhooded,
And what he hath taken he never lets go."

## A SERVIAN BEAUTY.

IS the Kolo* that dances before the
    white house,
And 't is Stoian's fair sister, O fair,
    fair is she!

---

* *Kolo*, signifying literally a wheel, is the generic term for
all the Servian national dances ; in most of which the dancers, either taking hands, or united each to each by a handkerchief tied round the waist or to the girdle, form a ring
and advance or retreat to and from the centre to a monotonous music, either of the voice or some very simple wind
instruments. Both sexes take part in these dances, which
are frequently in the open air.

Too fair she is truly, too fair, heaven knows,
(God forgive her !) so cruel to be.
The fair Vila, whom the wan clouds fondly
follow
O'er the mountain wherever she roam it,
Is not fairer nor whiter than she.
Her long soft eyelash is the wing of the swal-
low
When the dew of the dawn trembles from it,
And as dawn-stars her blue eyes to me ;
Her eyebrows so dark are the slender sea-
leeches ; *
Her rich-blooméd cheeks are the ripe river
peaches,
Her teeth are white pearls from the sea ;
Her lips are two half-opened roses ;
And her breath the south-wind, which dis-
closes
The sweetness that soothes the wild bee.
She is tall as the larch, she is slender
As any green bough the birds move ;
See her dance, — 't is the peacock's full splen-
dor !

---

* A strange, but very frequent, simile in Servian poetry.

Hear her talk, — 't is the coo of the dove !
And, only but let her look tender, —
'T is all heaven melting down from above !


## A DISCREET YOUNG WOMAN.

MILITZA has long soft eyelashes,
So darkly dreaming droopt on either
cheek,
You scarce can guess what little lightning
flashes
From those deep eyes, beneath them beaming,
break.
And her fair face, like a flower,
Has such drooping ways about it,
I have watcht her, many an hour,
Three full years, (O never doubt it ! )
And yet never have seen fairly
Eyes or face, — revealed so rarely !

Only just to rob one glance
From the happy grass beneath her,
On the green where maidens dance

When the month makes merry weather,
I the Kolo called together,
Trusting to my happy chance.
While the dance grew sweeter, faster
(Bosoms heaving, tresses shaken),
Suddenly with dim disaster
All the sky was overtaken.
Rolling darkness drowned the sunlight,
Rolling thunder drencht the valleys,
And in heaven was left but one light
From the lightning's livid sallies.

Like a necklace lightly shattered,
Shedding rubies, shedding pearls,
Here and there the Kolo scattered
All its bevy of bright girls.
Little, darling, timid creatures!
Each, with frightened, fluttered features,
Lifted up her pretty eyes
To the tempest growling o'er her;
But Militza, very wise,
Still kept looking straight before her.

Little voices, silvery, wild,
All at once, in fretful cadence,

Brake out chiding the sweet child.
" What, Militza ! " cried the maidens,
" Those grass-grazing eyes, I wonder,
From the ground can nothing startle?
Hark, child! how it groans, the thunder!
See! the lightnings, how they dartle
Here and there by angry fits,
In and out the stormy weather !
Hast thou wholly lost thy wits,
Little fool ?   Or must we deem
Thou wouldst something wiser seem
Than the whole world put together ? "

But Militza answers ... " Neither
Have I lost my wits, nor grown
Wiser, maidens, I must own,
Than the whole world put together.
I am not the Vila white,
Who, amidst her mountain ranges,
Lifting looks of stormy light,
Through his fifty moody changes,
Wooes the tempest's troubled sprite
Down the mountain melting o'er her, —
I am not a Vila white,
But a girl that looks before her."

## BOLOZÀNOVITCH, THE KNAVE.

JOUL,* the Turk, on a morning in
May,
When every bird is brilliant in feather,
And every flower in blossom is gay,
To celebrate sweetly the merry May weather,
From dawn to dusk, in dance and play,
Called a hundred matrons and maids together.
And the fairest maiden of all, that day,
Was the maid Bolozànovitch loved, they say.

He sought her all a summer noon,
And on to eventide;
He sought her under the summer moon,
Through all the country wide,
Till at nightfall he came, in the mist and murk,
To the lighted house of Djoul, the Turk.

" Djoul, Djoul with the raven hair!
Give me a shift of linen fair,

---

* For *Gul*, the Turk word, meaning *rose*.

Such as thyself art wont to wear
On the day when the glad new moon is born;
Paint me the eyebrow with antimony;
These bronzéd cheeks with white and red
Color; and comb me, and curl me the head;
Hang me over the shoulders free
Silken tresses two or three,
Such as by matron or maid are worn;
Bind me the brow with a golden braid,
And clothe me, anon, in the clothes of a maid
From head to foot, with many a fold
Of the milk-white tunic flowing and full;
And give me a distaff of gold
And a ball of Egyptian wool;
Then suffer me thus mid the maidens to move,
That I may speak to the maiden I love."

Djoul, the Turk with the raven hair,
Laught as she listened, and granted his prayer.
She clothed him in clothes of a maid,
Combed him and curled him the hair,
Painted his dark face fair,
Over his long limbs laid
Many a milk-white fold
Of vesture flowing and full;

Then gave him a distaff of gold,
And a ball of Egyptian wool ;
And when he was trickt and pincht and padded
And painted and plastered, to look like a lass,
Because he yet lookt like the knave that he
      was,
This good counsel she added :

" Bolozànovitch, knave, take note!
When anon, mid our women ye stand,
The old women take by the haud,
And kiss on their finger-tips ;
The young women kiss on the lips ;
But, for those that are maidens and girls,
You shall kiss them under the throat,
And over the collar of pearls."

Bolozànovitch gladly (the knave!)
Gave heed to the counsel she gave,
And of all, as she bade him, took note.
The old women each on the finger-tips
He kist, and the young women each on the lips,
And the maidens under the throat.

Maidenlike thus mid the maidens he moved,
Drooping the eyelid over the ground ;

But when he came to the maiden he loved,
He made her a little red wound
Just in the soft white fold
Of her slender throat.    Then she
Cried out to the women around,
"Strike! strike, with your distaffs of gold,
The knave who has wounded me!
For this was not a woman.    Behold,
'T is the knave Bolozànovitch, he!"


## THE WIFE OF HASSAN AGA.*

HAT is it so white on the mountain
    green?
    A flight of swans? or a fall of snow?
The swans would have flown, and the snow
    would have been
Melted away long ago.

---

* This poem was translated by Goethe into German, in
1789, from an Italian translation published by the Abbé
Fortis in 1774; and was thus the first of these national
songs and legends that ever passed from Servia into more
civilized lands.  Goethe's translation (Klaggesang von der
edeln Fraun dos Asan Aga) is unrhymed and remarkably
literal.

It is neither snow-fall, nor yet swan-flight.
But the tent of Hassan Aga so white.
Sore was the wound which in battle he got,
His mother and sister (for these without blame
Might do as they listed) to visit him came ;
But his wife, for the modest-minded shame
Of a matron chaste, could not.

Wherefore, when he had healed him his wound
   so sore,
Angered he said to his faithful spouse :
" Meet me no more, see me no more,
Mid our children, within my white house."
He frowned and he rode away.
Silent with deep dismay,
The Turkish woman wept,
Bitterly wept at her husband's word,
Clothed herself with sorrow, and crept
Into her chamber, and covered her brows,
When the hoof of a horse was heard
At the door of the Aga's house.

The fair Aguinitza * fled trembling away

---

* The wife of an Aga ; as *Pachinitza*, wife of a Pacha.

To the window, to fling herself down in her
    fear :
Her two little daughters came running, and they
Cried, "Mother, come back, mother dear !
For it is not our father Hassan is here,
But our uncle Pintorovitch Bey."

Back she turned, faltering she came,
Weeping she fell on the breast of her brother,
And . . . "O my brother," . . . she cried . . .
    "the shame,
From her children to sever a mother ! "

The Bey held silence, nor answered a word,
His smile was stern, but his eyes were dim,
As he drew from his silken pouch, and laid
In the hands of his sister, the letter which said
That her dower to her should, in full, be re-
    stored,
And she should return to their mother with
    him ! *
When the fair Turk that letter had read,
Her children she called to her one by one,

---

* The writing of divorce.

She kist her two boys on the brow and cheek ·
She kist her two girls on their lips' young red :
But when to the little one, lying alone
In the little cradle, she came,
The little one smiled as he slept :
Her heart began to break
With an inward anguish of shame :
She could neither move nor speak :
She sat down by the cradle and wept.

Then her brother Pintorovitch Bey
Drew softly the cradle away,
Lifted her into the saddle behind,
Turned, as he mounted, and kist her,
And rode off to his house with his sister,
Over the hills, in the wind.

Not long in the house of her mother
She rested ; not even a week.
Lovers, one after the other,
Came riding to sue and to seek :
For never more lovely a lady
Breathed beauty to trouble the land,
And soon from Imoski the Kadi
Came gayly to ask for her hand.

"O spare me, O save me, my brother!
My poor heart in sunder is reft :
My poor eyes are full of old tears :
Let me not be the bride of another,
For the sake of my little ones left,
For the sake of the once happy years."

But of all this full lightly he thought,
And he gave to the Kadi her hand :
Then sadly the Bey she besought,
And moaning she made her demand, —
On a fair paper, pure white,
These words to Imoski to write :

"*Fair greeting, in fair courtesy,
From her that hath been given to thee,
And courtesy to her prayer!
When the noble Svats \* assembled be,*

---

\* The Servian ceremonial of marriage is very peculiar.
On the wedding-day the bridegroom proceeds to the house of
the bride, accompanied by the guests, of both sexes, who attend the marriage on *his* invitation ; and who in this capac-
ity (of guests or witnesses) are called *Svats.*   He is sup-
ported by a *Koum,* or Best-man, a *Stari Svat,* or chief guest
(the oldest and most honored of the company), who attest
the marriage, and a *Derer* (paranymph or groomsman), which

*And ye come in a noble company*
*From her white house to carry thy bride,*
*Bring ye a long white covering fair*
*To cover her eyes ; that so, when ye ride*
*Beside the white house of the Aga, she*
*May see not her little ones there."*
When this letter was come to the Kadi's hand,
He assembled the noblest Svats of the land ;
And they all in a noble company rode
To carry the bride from her white abode.
Gayly to seek her they started,
And with her they gayly departed.
But, when they were merrily riding before
The Aga's white house, from the window at
   once

---

latter personage may be a married man. These receive the
bride from the hands of her parents, and are bound not to
lose sight of her till she enters her new home. All partici-
pation in the nuptial ceremonial is interdicted by custom to
the parents of the bride, who do not again behold their
daughter until eight days after the marriage. A mother,
indeed, cannot, compatibly with established usage, attend,
or be near, her daughter in child-bed. By being groomsman
or witness to a marriage, a relationship is contracted with
the bride's family of a nature so close and so strict as to be
deemed incompatible with marriage at any future period between the groomsman and any member of that family.

Lookt her two little daughters; her two little
  sons
Came running to her from the door,
And ... "Come back, mother dear, with us,
  come!
For dinner is waiting at home."

Then, weeping, the twice-wedded spouse
To the bold Stari Svat, ... "Dear, my brother
  in God,
For the dear love of God, pass not by this
  abode!
Let the horses wait here by the house;
That I, ere I see them no more,
(My dear ones, my little ones, see them no
  more!)
May speak, though it be but a while."
And the horses stopt straightway, and stood by
  the door,
And she past through the door with a smile.
Gay gifts to her children she gave:
To both of her boys bold and brave
Golden jatagans rich, and to both
Of her girls a long tunic of cloth.
But when to the little one, lying alone

In the cradle, she came, she laid mournfully on
The small cradle a white orphan garment,
A little white garment, and sighed,
And turned from the cradle wild-eyed,
With looks of despairing endearment.

All of this Hassan Aga espied,
And he turned to his two sons, and cried,
" Little orphans, come here ! come to me !
For pitiless, children, is she,
Your mother stone-hearted, the bride ! "

Cruel, cruel and keen was the word!
Silent she listened and heard,
Heard the harsh word that he said.
To the black earth she bowed her bright head :
She had not another reply,
Than to droop her white forehead, and die :
For the heart of the mother was broken in twain
For the love, and the loss, of her little ones ta'en.

## SLEEPLESSNESS.

LEEP will not take the place of Love,
    Nor keep the place from Sorrow.
    O, when the long nights slowly move
To meet a lonely morrow,
The burthen of the broken days,
The grief that on the bosom weighs,
And all the heart oppresses,
But lightly lies on restless eyes
Love seals no more with kisses.

## NEGLECTED FLOWERS.

ITTLE violet, drooping all alone, like
    my own
    Drooping heart, I would pluck thee;
    but there 's none, no not one!
To whom I dare to give thee : so I leave thee,
    and pass on.
I would give thee gladly, gladly, if I dared, to
    Ali Bey;

But too proud (ah well-a-day!) is Ali Bey, —
    so they say!
Proud he is! I do not dare. Would he care,
    he to wear
Any flower that buds or blows? ... save the
    rose, I suppose!
No! rest there, and despair! Live or die!
    Thou and I
Have no chance to catch one glance from his
    eye, passing by.


## PLUCKING A FLOWER.

### HE.

MAIDEN, vermeil rose!
Unplanted, unsown,
Blooming alone
As the wild-flower blows,
With a will of thine own!
Neither grafted nor grown,
Neither gathered nor blown,
O maiden, O rose!
Blooming alone

In the green garden-close,
Unnoticed, unknown,
Unpropt, unsupported,
Unwatered, unfed,
Unkist, and uncourted,
Unwooed, and unwed,
O sweet wild rose,
Who knows? Who knows?
Might I kiss thee, and court thee?
My kiss would not hurt thee!
O sweet, sweet rose,
In the green garden-close,
If a gate were undone,
And if I might come to thee,
And meet thee alone?
Sue thee, and woo thee,
And make thee my own?
Clasp thee, and cull thee, — what harm would
    be done?

### SHE.

Beside thy field my garden blows.
Were a gate in the garden left open . . . who
    knows?
And I watered my garden at eventide?

(Who knows ?)
And if somebody silently happened to ride
That way ?   And a horse to the gate should be
    tied ?
And if somebody, (who knows who ?) unespied,
Were to enter my garden to gather a rose ?
Who knows ? . . . I suppose
No harm need be done.   My belovéd one,
Come lightly, come softly, at set of the sun !
Come, and caress me !
Kiss me, and press me !
Fold me, and hold me !
Kiss me with kisses that leave not a trace,
But set not the print of thy teeth on my face,
Or my mother will see it, and scold me.


## TRANSPLANTING A FLOWER.

MAIDEN, mother's golden treasure !
Purest gold of perfect pleasure !
Do they beat thee, and ill-treat thee,
That I meet thee all alone ?
Do they beat thee, that I meet thee

All too often, all too late,
After nightfall, at the gate
Of the garden, all alone ?
Tell me, tell me, little one,
Do they do it ?   If I knew it,
They should rue it!   I would come
Oftener, later, yet again,
(Hail, or snow, or wind, or rain !)
Oftener, later !   Nor in vain :
For if mother, for my sake,
Were to drive thee out of home,
Just three little steps 't would take
(Think upon it, little one ! ) —
Just three little steps, or four,
To my door from mother's door.
Love is wise.   I say no more.
Ponder on it, little one !


## A MESSAGE.

WEET sister of my loved, unloving one,
 Kiss thy wild brother, kiss him ten-
       derly !
Ask him what is it, witless, I have done

That he should look so coldly upon me?
Ah, well ... I know he recks not! Let it be.
Yet say ... "There's many a woodland nod-
　　ding yet
For who needs wood when winter nights be
　　cold."
Say ... "Love to give finds ever love to get.
There lack not goldsmiths where there lacks not
　　gold.
The wood will claim the woodman by and by;
The gold (be sure!) the goldsmith cannot miss;
Each maid to win finds lads to woo: and I ... "
Well, child, but only tell him, tell him this!
Sweet sister, tell him this!


## ISOLATION.

THE night is very dark and very lonely:
　　And as dark, and all as lonely, is my
　　　heart:
And the sorrow that is in it night knows only:
For the dawn breaks, and my heart breaks.
　　　Far apart

From my old self seems my new self.  And my
    mother
And my sister are in heaven, — so they say:
And the dear one dearer yet than any other
Is far, far away.
The sweet hour of his coming ... night is fall-
    ing!
The hour of our awakening ... bird on bough!
The hour of last embraces ... friends are calling!
"Love, farewell!" ... and every hour is silent
    now.

## A REGRET.

LOST empire of my maidenhood!
    Could I be once more what I would,
    Then what I am I would not be.
Ah, well-a-day, and woe is me!
Could I a maiden be once more,
And unknow all that I have known,
And feel as I have felt of yore,
I would not change with any queen
Not for sceptre, crown, or throne,

If I could be what I have been
Would I grow what I have grown.

Lost empire of my maidenhood!
Sweetest sweet! and chiefest good!
Now that thou art gone, I know,
Could I call thee back again,
How to keep thee.   Even so!
Loss is all my gain!

Would that I were with the flocks
As of old among the rocks!
For the flocks do blithely bleat,
And the mountain airs blow sweet,
And the river runneth fleet,
Running to the happy sea:
But the glory of the river,
And the gladness of the flocks,
And the mirth among the rocks,
And the music on the wind
Ministrant to a merry mind, —
These are joyous things, forever
Dead, or fled, for me!

On the wind there moans forever
One word only, which the river,

Murmuring, murmurs to the shore,
And the flocks, with chilly bleat,
Evermore that word repeat,
And that word is — Nevermore!
Nevermore, O never, never
Any more, by mount or river,
Shall I be as I have been,
A mountain maid, a virgin queen!


## THE BAN OF VARADIN.

WASSAILER in wildest ways,
But foul befall the churl who says
That what he drinks he never pays,
So mad a devil dwells within
The brain of Peter Doïtchin,
The burly Ban of Varadin! *

Three hundred ducats in a day
Good sooth, he swilled them all away!
And, when he had no more to pay,

---

* Servian name for Petervardein, fortress in Hungary.

First his massy mace of gold,
Then his coal-black horse he sold.
" Fill up the can, keep out the cold,
And let the merry devil in,
Sweetheart ! " laught Peter Doïtchin,
The burly Ban of Varadin !

Quoth King Mathias* . . . " Burly Ban,
God curse thee for a brainless man,
Whose goods flow from him in the can !
Three hundred ducats in a day,
Thou hast swilled them all away,
And, for lack of more to pay,
Thou thy massy mace of gold,
And thy coal-black war-steed bold,
For a sorry stoup hast sold."

" King Mathias, cease thy prattle !
Brainless heads are hard in battle :
Fighting men make thirsty cattle.
Hadst thou the tavern drained with me,
The tavern wench upon thy knee,
(So sweet and sound a wench is she !)

* Probably Mathias Corvinus.

Thou wouldst have drunk up thy good town
Of Pesth, with Buda tower and down,
Camp, acropolis, court, and crown!"

## FATIMA AND MEHMED.

ENEATH a milk-white almond-tree,
Fatima and Mehmed be.
The black earth is their bridal bed;
The thick-starréd sky clear-spread
Is their coverlet all the night,
As they lie in each other's arms so white.
The grass is full of honey-dew;
The crescent moon, that glimmers through
The unrippled leaves, is faint and new:
And the milk-white almond blossoms
All night long fall on their bosoms.

Cambridge: Printed by Welch, Bigelow, & Co.